THE STORY OF GRAYBO AND POSSUM

Lester Betts

ISBN 979-8-88751-635-6 (paperback)
ISBN 979-8-88751-636-3 (digital)

Copyright © 2023 by Lester Betts

All rights reserved. No part of this publication may be reproduced, distributed, or transmitted in any form or by any means, including photocopying, recording, or other electronic or mechanical methods without the prior written permission of the publisher. For permission requests, solicit the publisher via the address below.

Christian Faith Publishing
832 Park Avenue
Meadville, PA 16335
www.christianfaithpublishing.com

Pictures by Helen Betts

Printed in the United States of America

To my wife, Helen Betts, and to all
the animal lovers around the world.

Born April 2014 in Lucasville, Ohio, Graybo is one of three kittens of our cat Calico. We gave two away. Graybo is like in color as her mother, Calico. She is all gray with a bushy tail. She is lots of fun for us.

She takes flea baths along with Possum, which I will get to later.

She is always playing and, at night, likes to paw the pillow and blankets.

Graybo's mother, Calico, has been with us for five years. She is a calico. We do not know who Graybo's dad is, but we love her. She is always full of fun and running around the house.

Now that brings us around to her little friend she spends all day and night with, Possum.

Possum is around the same age as Graybo. Possum was born in West Portsmouth, Ohio. Possum was given to us by my wife's friend, Pam. He is a gray like her and has a bushy tail. He has four white feet and a white belly.

Possum's mother was like him. He also had two sisters. Possum is a Persian-like kitten. Possum is very handsome for a boy, and Graybo thinks so too.

These two kittens play all the time together. They love to get treats and play outside.

Outside, they chase butterflies

and, at night, they jump up and chase fireflies.

Both kittens are four months old now, and I need to get them to the vet for all their shots.

Graybo likes to watch TV. Possum likes to chase the arrow on the computer screen.

Someday, we hope they will have some kittens of their own. That would be nice. Who knows? They might even get married. We could buy them matching flea collars, and that could be their wedding rings.

ABOUT THE AUTHOR

It all started in 1945 in Pickaway County, Ohio. Lester Betts was born. He attended Salt Creek School for nine years and graduated from Logan Elm.

Born on a farm, I drove trucks most of my life. The love of animals inspired me to write this book. The kittens are grown up now but are a lot of joy.

Printed in the USA
CPSIA information can be obtained
at www.ICGtesting.com
LVHW071204261023
762204LV00017B/544